For Carly
you should be here
to read these words
you helped guide me
you changed my world

SANDRA COOPER

Thank you

To my sweetheart
for loving me all the times
I was falling apart

To my ma and pa
for making the vast distance
between us feel small

To my "little" bro
for always celebrating me
and helping me grow

To those who believed in me
for helping me see
all I could be

Sandra Cooper

Author's Note

For as long as I can remember, writing has been my passion. My anchor in a storm, my companion in a lonely world. During the hardest times of my life, I continuously find myself with notebook and pen in hand, feverishly, desperately trying to make sense of my feelings through poems, stories, and journal entries.

This collection was written when I was trapped in depression, drowning in my own pity. From this terrifying **stillness** I learned to breathe again, slowly but surely. Using words as my guides, I began to feel lighter, finally able to **move** again. These small waves ignited my **fire** and reminded me of my creative powers and their transformational abilities. Steaming with emotions stirred by the fire, I emerged into a **flow** state. I opened myself up to the rocky stream of life, eventually anchoring in a forgotten place of strength and resilience. Surrounded by loved ones, I returned **home**. Upon my return it seemed that everything had changed and yet the **elements** stayed the same.

I share the tender parts of my soul in the hopes that this work speaks to you and provides some small amount of comfort, should you find yourself in dire straits. Buckle in and enjoy your journey.

SANDRA COOPER

ELEMENTS

Table of Elements

Space

$\hspace{12cm}$ 1

Air

$\hspace{12cm}$ 23

Fire

$\hspace{12cm}$ 45

Water

$\hspace{12cm}$ 67

Earth

$\hspace{12cm}$ 89

Elements

$\hspace{12cm}$ 123

Sandra Cooper

ELEMENTS

These words

                        levitate

                                              in my soul

I hesitate

                to translate them

                                    in a way that will

                    resonate

Sandra Cooper

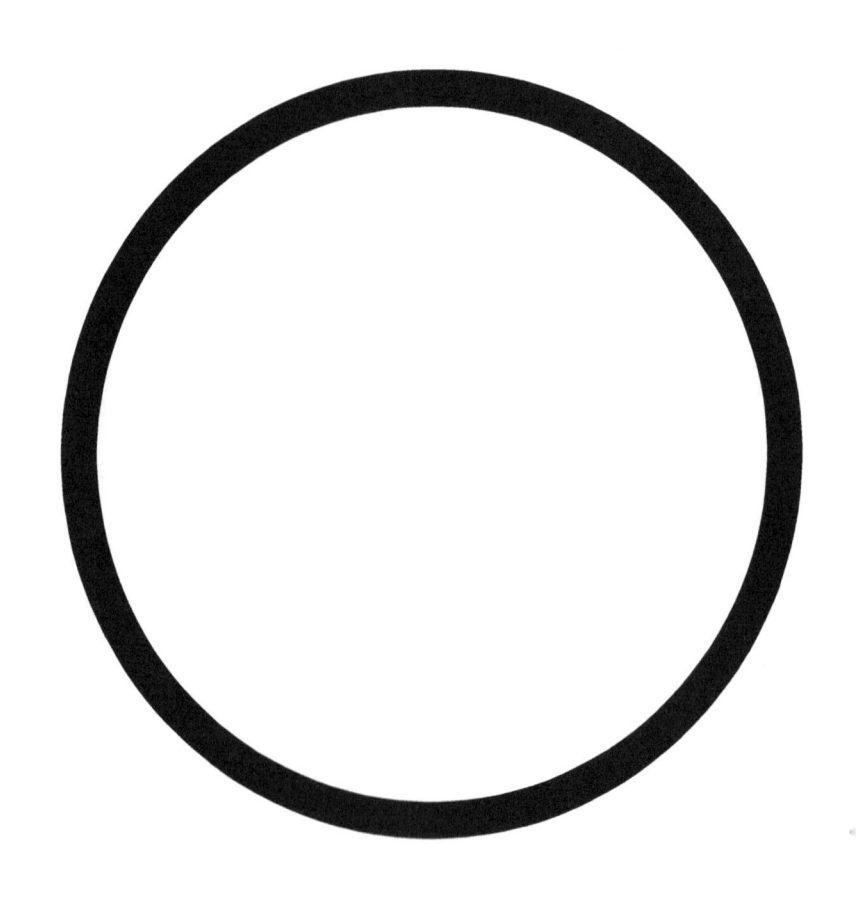

ELEMENTS

SPACE

Sandra Cooper

Stillness

*I am
as still
as the vast
emptiness
that was
space
before
movement.
In the
stillness,
the darkness,
the emptiness,
much is born
in the mind,
there are many
movements unseen;
thus began
my journey
into light.
I came
from
stillness
darkness
emptiness.*

Even on dark days...
On the gloomiest days -
and you will just have to
believe me on this -
on the gloomiest days
there are still
infinite reasons
to feel grateful
even if they're
stupid reasons
like
the smell of coffee
the way your dog sings
the feeling of sunshine
on your bare skin
light only comes in
if you let it
just know
it is always there
even on
the gloomiest days

Feblueary
Dark days outside
reflected inside
I am
as dark as
the world I see
through my windows

Dark days
long nights
losing sight
of why I
should fight
can't make
my mind right

I want to stay
deep inside
this warm
cozy bed
it is the only place
that feels safe
on days when
I only feel
the dark side
of myself

Sandra Cooper

I never knew how much
courage it takes to
quietly endure unyielding pain
putting on a brave face
just to face the day
takes a lifetime worth of strength

I have become unraveled
having to pretend
I am not falling apart
hopeless and defeated

it is exhausting
to repeat and repeat and repeat
to every person I see
why I am not
my usual happy, positive self

so I pretend to be fine
and I smile when it hurts
and I laugh so I don't cry
and all the while

I am trying not to
completely fall apart
and all the while
I keep my pain
dressed up nicely
>> ***it's easier than telling my story***

ELEMENTS

I crave the darkness so strongly
each drop of light that pierces my skin
sends me further down the rabbit hole
of my infinite soul

I want to consume the light
until my soul becomes a stone
heavy and burdened under the weight
of my own existence

isn't that what complete obscurity teaches us?
To be afraid of the light?
It teaches us to embrace the inevitable
heaviness that pulls us tight

I will happily dive deeper
into this rabbit hole of dark insanity
most of us play it safe
seeing only in the light of day

treading only into the patches of sunshine
stitched between rows of dark clouds
not knowing that we are missing
exactly half of life

play in the light all you want
you are only increasing the hold
the darkness has on you

There is a wiggle in my mind
that comes out through my feet
mom always thought I just
loved to dance, not realizing
I was freeing my mind from
the nonstop jitterbug
the eternal foxtrot of thoughts
that parade on repeat
back and forth ceaselessly
across the stage of my mind

There is a fizzle in my mind
that comes out through my fingers
dad always thought I just
loved to write, not realizing
I was releasing my mind from
an endless script
an infinite monologue
about nothing
that scrolls and scribes relentlessly
across the pages of my mind

Believing
is a dangerously potent
medicine
just ask those
who don't
          Choose to believe in something

I tried it
not caring
pretending to be okay
giving up

I tried it
not trying
not taking care
not looking for joy

I did it for a long time
I tried being miserable
I wore it like a new skin
maybe that is why
I was always itchy

maybe part of me always knew
there was more out there for me
than misery and suffering
and if I used my power
of choosing

I could choose
to try hard
to show up
to care
to look for joy

and maybe eventually
I would see that whatever
I look for is what I see

and maybe eventually
I will learn to only look for
the good parts
to only see the progress
and ignore
the journey yet to come

maybe eventually
I will come to see
I am worthy of
the most attention
the finest care
the gentlest touch

and I will let go of
not feeling like enough

I know what you want to hear from me
I will save you the time and tell you now
I am not the little girl you knew
I am not who you want me to be

somewhere along the way I got hurt
and broken in ways I could not explain
the hurt piled up into dark messy spaces
that I always worried you would unearth

so I distanced myself
changed everything but my name
part of me hoped that when I left home
home would leave me alone

I was wrong, so so naïvely wrong
me being further away
just made you want to be closer
the umbilical cord trying to hang on

I know what you want to hear from me
you won't
I cannot love you the way you need me to
but I need you to keep loving me

I know love is a two way street
my heart cannot beat strongly enough
for all of us so I chose me
me loving me more means loving you less

ELEMENTS

no it is not fair after all you have built
after the nest you kept for all those years
how dare I not be able to offer you the same
loving attention and affection, a connection?

I put up walls against those who attempted
to see me for my real self
taking my shame off the shelf and wearing it
trying to hide as someone else

it is inconceivable
this notion of being a death potion
for your parents' love and attention
they can fix anything with love

and I can't even
show them I care

Rent Overdue
Distracted
by obsessive thoughts
misunderstanding
my own mind

it is exhausting to feel
like I am overdue on rent
in my own body, not big enough
for the space I am occupying

these arms are
too thin and
cannot hold the weight
of a life I have outgrown

Elements

Follow those trains of thought
those times that your intuition
is playing peek-a-boo
with your consciousness;
you never know where
you might meet yourself

While you are busy worrying
what they are thinking
about you,
they are busy worrying
what you are thinking
about them
stop the madness
and let yourself think
about something worth
thinking about

the mind is the place
after all, you see,
where journeys begin
without leaving your seat
it can be used to create
the most magical ways
of seeing doing making
and yet for many days
you have been fretting,
forgetting your power
lies in your mind
you are wasting time

take back control
tell her who's boss
own that mind of yours
all hope ain't lost

How to Get What you Want

Practice *loving yourself* in moments of loneliness
practice saying *I am brave* in moments of fear
practice *showing up* in moments of anger
practice the art of practicing

nothing
not one thing
in life
comes without
practice

talk all you want
about what you want
if you do not practice
having it
you will never have it

After all,
rock bottom is not
the worst place
you could find yourself
at least you know
it is as bad as
it can possibly get
now you can look
forward to
climbing out.

No matter how much
you get hurt
there is something valuable
to be learned from
the journey.

Appreciate how
awful it feels
to be at your worst
that way next time,
you will not be surprised.

Elements

"I am doing my best"
repeat daily as needed
to yourself until
you start to believe it

Why Does it Matter What I Think?

Let's talk thoughts. Many people have said it many ways and let me be one more, *you are what you think*. Whatever you are constantly telling yourself becomes true. Your truth is different from my truth is different from her truth is different from their truth because what we tell ourselves becomes the truth. If I constantly tell myself, "I am ugly. I am not pretty. I am not beautiful." that becomes my truth, my reality. Someone else, anyone else, may see me and think, "She is not ugly, she is pretty. She is beautiful." and that is their truth, their reality. Whatever you are thinking about, whatever you are telling yourself (which are really the same thing) is true. **Choose wisely the words you repeat to yourself**. Choose wisely the patterns you are creating in your mind. This is the only thing you have control over in your entire lifetime, your whole existence. Everything comes down to your ability to realize you have control over your mind, and when you control your mind you control your life. It sounds silly because of how simple it is. Practice telling yourself loving thoughts, practice talking to yourself how you want to be spoken to. Practice being the person you most admire and soon enough you will admire yourself. Practice believing you have the power to be in control of your mind. Sure, if you would prefer, you can let your mind do all of the controlling. See how that works out for you, let me know. I can make a pretty solid guess that you will never regain control. Once you've admitted defeat, once you've waved the white flag of retreat, once you've given up the driver's seat, you've already written your last heartbeat.

Sandra Cooper

ELEMENTS

AIR

ELEMENTS

Moving

*I had to
abandon
the stillness
and walk slowly
into
a part of
myself
I had always
neglected.
I silently agreed
to the
exploration
of my
heartspace.
I moved slowly
through the
soft darkness
that enveloped
my heart
and encouraged it
gently
to open enough
to let me in.*

Overcome
It does not matter
what your struggle is
what it looks like
if you struggle
it means you are alive
I do not care
if your struggle looks like
battle after incessant battle

>   *you get up and fight*

I do not care
if your struggle looks like
being shattered and having to
put a million pieces back together

>   *you get to gluing*

You have the capacity
to overcome any battle
that you believe you have
the capacity to overcome

>   **I'll say it again**

You have the ability
to overcome any fight
that you believe you have
the ability to overcome

The limiting factor becomes
the mind
don't let that silly one
in the driver's seat.

Above All
Do it for you
let yourself in
to your own life
how can you expect
other people
to show up for you
if you do not
show up
for yourself?
Learn how to be patient
with yourself first
so you can be patient
with others
learn to accept love
from yourself first
so you can accept love
from others
be the example for others
of how
you are to be treated
with love
kindness
patience
respect
from you
to you
first
and above all

If your victory today
looks like making the bed
then you make the shit
out of that bed

If your victory today
means walking laps
around the house
you walk those fucking laps

If miracles happened daily
they would be meaningless
sometimes doing your best
means doing almost nothing
> ***Celebrate every victory***

Fuck What Yoda Said
The truth is
nobody knows
what the fuck
they are doing
we are all
just guessing
all the time
pretending
taking risks
offending
making mistakes
judging
sometimes winning
stumbling
getting up
trying
again.
You are not meant
to have a clue
as to
what the fuck
you are doing
just
                       try
                                           anyway.
Enjoy
                       the
                                           ride.

I must hate myself
right?
If I feel the need to
feed myself with
poisonous foods
toxic media
destructive relationships
I must hate myself.
People who love themselves do not
treat themselves like this
right?

Who can I look to
for a good example of
loving myself?
Is it my mother,
the stunning successful seductress
who calls herself
by the very names her brothers
taunted her with in her youth
so that decades later she
still believes she
is not worthy she
still believes she
is not beautiful how
can I use her as an example of
loving myself?

ELEMENTS

Or perhaps my father,
the enthusiastic earnest entrepreneur
who sees himself
as less than
no matter how great
he is at whatever project he
is working on he
feels unsuccessful he
cannot see his value he
feels like a castaway
should he be my example of
loving myself?

You are what you eat
and see and hear
your entire life
try to ingest love
inspiration joy goodness
if nobody taught you
how to love yourself
you will just have to
teach yourself
and what a gift it is
to have the capacity to learn
and the capacity
to love

It is not too late to learn to love

Inhale, Exhale

Life only exists
in a conscious moment
so whether you are
suffering deeply or
purely elated, you
are eternally living
one breath at a time
if it feels unbearable
slow the breath down
focus on it
draw the moment out
and remember it
as a conscious moment
of existence
pure existence
no joy or suffering
just you and your breath
you only have to endure
one breath
at a time

Control

Do not allow me
to decide who you are
I will always try to tear you down
because you terrify me

do not allow me
to control how you feel
I will always try to invalidate you
because I cannot express myself

on this path I walk
each step is a lesson
with each step
I become closer to the person
I am designed to be

I stumble more times
than the steps I get right
I'm putting my best foot forward
despite what it looks like

everything is crafted, constructed
can you feel it?
Let go of control
and see where you end up
despite what you think
the car can steer itself

Impossible to tell where
my skin ends and the scales begin
I always thought
the shedding of my skin
would be painless and quick
like the basilisk
slithering through
her secret chamber.
I have been shedding this skin
for years and
nothing has changed
it still does not fit

living with psoriasis

Alchemy of Pain
You claim to
understand that
beauty and pain
are opposites and that
in order to see beauty you
have to feel pain you
say you
understand that
but then when
you are in the pain you
have lost the ability to
see beauty
and you forget that
pain is part of
the process
without it there is no
beauty to be seen so
relax and trust
relax and trust
relax and trust
beauty is the sun
do you think
he has an easy journey?
Sun continues to rise
even when you cannot see him
always following you
reminding you
beauty is born from pain

You can scratch all you want
the itch will never disappear
you can cry all you want
the pain will never clear

You have to
find the source
of the itch
of the pain

If you treat the symptom
the disease will grow
find the cause
find the cure

Elements

it is not about who
you are with
it is who you are asking
them to be with
love yourself so they can love you

He looks
at her
the way
the moon
looks at
the sun

I want that

Breathing had always come
naturally
my breath and I were
friends
until my lungs stopped
cooperating
and my breath started
catching
in my throat

I can't remember who
betrayed
who but my breath and I became
strangers
no longer able to
flow
as one

Slowly, patiently I called her
back
in small quiet hours I made
space
in my body so she would feel welcome

at home

Forgetting to Feel
Do you remember in school
learning to draw hands on clocks?
Do you remember learning
colours with chalk
and patterns on the sidewalk?

Do you remember learning
to match words like
afraid, angry, happy, playful
to drawings of cartoon faces?

We learned all of these words
for emotions and feelings
sadness, fear, confusion,
it left my mind reeling

Now all these years later
it seems we only remember
happy as **landlord**
all others as *renters*

We betray ourselves
by pretending the presence
of each of our feelings
is less than perfection.

Quiet Love
I used to think it mattered
how many people were invited
to my birthday party,
not really caring
how many of them came,
just wanting the public guest list
to be loud and impressive
"Look how many people
I barely know"
the list gushed, crying
out for attention
just as much as me

Now I realize how much time
I wasted trying to build
the biggest, widest, least stable web
composed of tenuous connections
that would have fallen apart
with the lightest touch.
Now I realize how much
better it feels to
fortify the connections that
helped me build the web
in the first place,
and so I've been practicing
loving the people who
have always loved me,
no matter how quietly.

Show Up and Face Your Shadow

What does showing up for yourself look like? Standing your ground when your intuition says to stay and fight. Speaking up when you see something that is not right. Trusting your way through darkness to light. Standing still enough to feel the beat of your heart when you're falling apart. Standing still enough to feel your intuition pulsing through your veins. Listening to the undeniable parts of yourself crying out in pain or frustration or rage. Showing up for yourself is a practice at the root of all practice. Building a practice is a practice in and of itself - and it requires a lot of showing up. Showing up regardless of how tired you are. Showing up regardless of how many emails you have unread. Showing up regardless of how bad your dreams were or the nasty thing your boss said. Showing up regardless of the pain in your body, the weakness in your mind, the dread in your heart. You know it is going to hurt - the stripping away of the comfort zone layers, the replacement of doubts with prayers. **Unlearning is uncomfortable and showing up is a practice**. Showing up is a practice and it is uncomfortably slow. You will fall and stumble and not know where you're going but life does not have one path laid out for you. It is up to you which path you stumble down, you get to choose. Choose wisely and choose foolishly. Choose often and choose well. Show up and choose, moment after moment, again and again, the life you want. That is what showing up for yourself looks like. Show up for yourself, moment after moment, again and again, for as long as you live, for that is the power of having control over your mind. Show up for yourself simply by showing up. You do not have to be the best. You have to be exactly nothing. Especially for anyone other than yourself. Simply be. You. *Show up for you.* You owe it to yourself to just show up. Show up and see what happens.

Sandra Cooper

ELEMENTS

FIRE

Sandra Cooper

ELEMENTS

Burning

*I can feel
that passion
burning bright
aching to bust out
and see the light
for the first time
feeling completely
alive
here
arrived
ready to begin
the journey of
a lifetime
guided by
that burning passion
ready for action
falling in love
with myself
from the inside out
facing the battle
ready to stand
my ground against
whatever monsters
lurk beneath
the reflective surface
of my shipwrecked
soul.*

Never Give Up
Each time I want
to give up
I remind myself
of almost not
reaching the summit
on that day
in the Alps
and if I
had given up
I would never
have seen the
most spectacular view
of my life
I would never
have felt the
edge of the
world at my
fingertips and I
would never
give that up
for anything

Elements

There is so much I want to say
a whole universe
bursts inside me, filling me
with vitality and joy

Yet every time
I put pen to paper
my mind goes blank
my thoughts play hide-and-seek

Showing up at
the most unlikely times
disappearing when I eventually
find time to record them

That's how it goes,
isn't it?
The great idea always
ends before it starts

She Writes in the Dark of Night

In the dark of night
is when she writes
stitching together
the missing pieces of herself
with words that comfort the hurt
she weaves a nest
using words and phrases
that she can feel safe in.

In her own world
she feels safe
in a world she
creates in her mind
nobody can touch her here
in her magic-making den
the setting, the characters, the plot
are all up to her.

She floats around
from thought to idea
picking some for further inspection
discarding the rest;
she rebuilds her lost soul
one story at a time
each story crafted
one word at a time.

ELEMENTS

Raw
vulnerable
not trying to be beautiful
trying to be real

learning
healing
afraid
courageous
I am human
making my way
through this life
one breath at a time

judge me?
not more than I have judged myself
hate me?
not more than I have hated myself
don't get me?
not more than I have misunderstood myself

your life is yours
mine is mine
we can be in it together
if we see ourselves
for who we are

Today is the Tomorrow from Yesterday
Each day is a chance
to do the things
that yesterday you said
you would do tomorrow

each day is
a chance to be
whichever imperfect version
of yourself
you have the capacity
to be

do your best
and accept that
each day
your best
will be different
from the last

Consumption
Sure by all means eat the junk food
do the drugs
watch the news
let your body get loose

It is not me you are offending
it is not my life you are affecting
by neglecting
to attend to your beautiful vessel

Your obligation is not to me
I could not care less what you eat
drink, wear, and read
those choices are yours alone

But don't you care about
how you feel?
Don't you pay attention
to the consequences of your choices?

What you consume
creates your entire being
consume whatever you want
to be

Singularity
One way, one idea, one thought
the alternatives do not exist
the edges of the box you
live in are too close to see
there is a name for it
when all dimensions are collapsed
into a single point
so you can no longer separate
one from the other:
singularity.
It is the same word used to describe
the phenomenon of man
becoming machine.
No other
no separation
oneness
Are you ready?
Are you ready to let go
and expand beyond
this single dimension?
You will only fly
if you release
your grip
on the ground.

ELEMENTS

Today's mantra:
My desire to be
who I know I *can* be
is greater than
my attachment to
who I *am*

In your Own Time
When you get tired of this act
when you grow tired of yourself
come find me

I have been observing you
growing weary
running in circles
not even knowing
what you're chasing

I have been watching you
growing impatient
letting the joy drain
from all that you do

when you are ready
come find me
for I have become somewhat
of an expert

on outgrowing oneself
I have outgrown my life
more times than I have been reborn

I am constantly in a state of
wanting things to change
being dissatisfied
feeling discontent

ELEMENTS

when you are willing
to be witness to your own death
and accept your rebirth
                come find me

I will be ready
to help you start again

Rather than simply dreaming about
the life you so greatly desire,
start living it and watch it
manifest perfectly
before your eyes

ELEMENTS

Climb one more ridge
hold on one more moment
speak one more truth
take one more breath
do not give up
before you have tried everything

You are Strong Enough
The hard days matter
just as much as the easy ones
maybe even more because
the hard days offer
endless opportunities for
learning and changing and
is that not the whole
point of life after all?
Do not get fooled into
thinking there is something
wrong with you for
having a hard time, it is
perfectly normal to feel
like your shit could not be
any less together, but
there is always a lesson
in the struggle, the suffer,
the heartbreak, the deep ache.
You can be a better
version of yourself if
you learn to appreciate
the hard days as
much as the easy ones.

Lesson Learned
It is hard to talk about how bad life has been
because writing about it makes it true, real.
It is easier when it is hidden inside,
left to rot and be used as an excuse
to treat myself and all around me
as badly as I feel

to write about it makes it come alive
a thing for me to take ownership of
to claim it and address it
and be better because of it

now is the time to put my game face on
decide how I want to keep living
pull up my socks and
finish this battle

the lesson to be learned
is in the learning of the lesson
I am done repeating mistakes
and missing the message
time to get learning
while the flame is still burning

As good as it may feel
to have so many weapons
in your self-sabotage arsenal
I promise you
it only feels good
because you are conditioned to that

As hard as it may be
to put down the weapons
to surrender the battle
I promise you
you do not need
such a strong defense
> ***learn to live without your shield***

Long story Short
Synopsis of your life:
(and everyone else's)
Be born
Struggle
Survive
Suffer
Survive
Sustain
Survive
Surrender
Die
Repeat

Transforming Beyond Recognition

It happened so slowly it was hard to notice at first. It made me wonder if butterflies noticed their cocoons opening. From that dark place of stillness, where I barely recognized myself, I made my first movements. I began, slowly, to face my fears and face myself. I did not always like what I saw or learned, but that was all part of this journey I did not agree to. I learned that, just as a fire dances any way it feels, my road to recovery would not follow any formula. It was time to take inventory of my strengths, build up my defenses and brace myself for the beast being unleashed by the internal barrier that had been broken. I was changed, transformed beyond recognition, having to make the impossible choice to let go of a life I had outgrown. I would stroll around, nude and vulnerable, until I found a new one that fit better. The fire that I could feel burning was unfamiliar and bred a new strain of fear I had to learn to swallow. I embodied the dragons I had watched playing out this scene my whole life, and I breathed fire onto everything I could see. The fire immediately destroyed any evidence of my existence. With quick licks it tarnished and burned, chewed up and digested every part of my past. Nothing was left to rebuild. If I thought my life had become unrecognizable during the storm, the aftermath was a different story. I wrote my name in the ashes of my previous self and closed the door gently as I walked out. Sweeping my shoes off on the doormat, I wanted to make sure I was leaving everything behind that was holding me back. It seemed I did not have a choice but to walk boldly into a new life that I hoped would fit better than the last. Lessons learned, pockets full of words, I marched next door and, although I knew nobody would be there, I knocked softly before letting myself in. Hello, brand new me. Lovely to finally meet you.

SANDRA COOPER

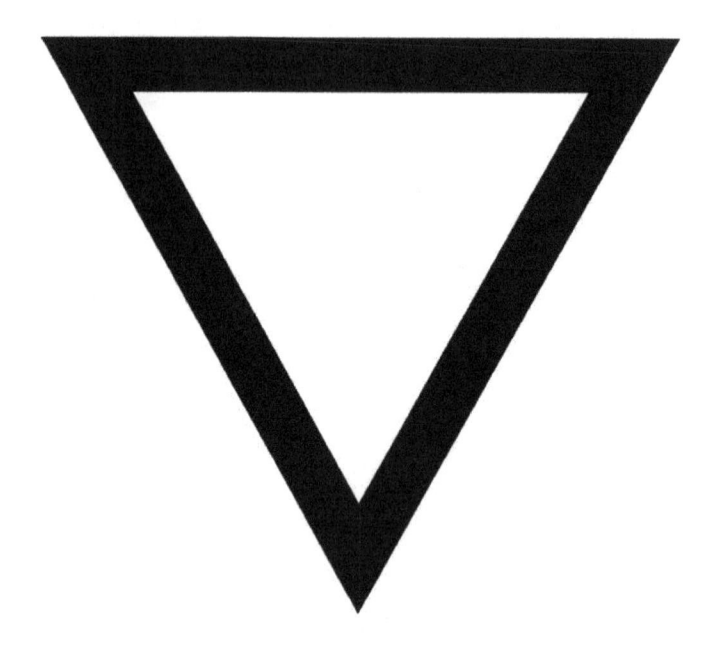

ELEMENTS

WATER

ELEMENTS

Flowing

*And only then
once I lay down my sword
let go of my fight
and learned to walk
with my pain
we started to work
together
and became
an unbreakable force
a raging waterfall
flowing effortlessly.
I was forged from
a fiery storm of
misunderstanding and great fear,
and these forces have melted
together to
recreate me.
As if emerging
from an eternal
sweat lodge
I found myself steaming
with feelings
both old and new
stirred by the storm
and I knew I was capable
of the work
I had to do.*

Dear Anxiety,
I know you want to be friends
so fucking badly
you knock at my door
call text and email
constantly
it's like you cannot live
without me

your incessant need
to show up
when you are least wanted
reminds me of
a pimple on picture day:
a surprise in the worst way.

it is not to say
you are not welcome
in my life
I know you serve a purpose
you hold some value
otherwise you would not exist

it is just your permanent
insistence we be best friends
that we spend
our whole existence together
you are too persistent

ELEMENTS

I do not need you
the way you need me
I have lived with you
and without you;
there is a life-sized difference
in my happiness
when you are not around.
I realize sadly I do not get to
make that choice

I want to
be in control, but
you decide
when to come and
when to go
you decide
how I am feeling
moment to moment

or at least
you have until now
I've made it easy for you
I have avoided you
I got out of your way
left you in control
I feared your power
which only gave you more
I resisted you
which only made you hungrier

no longer will I allow you
to follow me around
like a shadow
to mimic my own
voice so perfectly
that when you're
in my head
I can't tell
if it is me or you

no longer will I give you
the space to
manipulate me
the strength to
be in control

I am practicing acceptance
starting with me
as I am
scarred, damaged, awkward, and immature
I accept myself
unsure, in love, passionate, and stubborn
I love myself

if you and I come
as a package deal
then so be it
bring it on

Elements

give me all you've got
try your fucking worst
to make me fear you
I guarantee I will
reflect you so strongly
that you will begin to
fear yourself

for I have gotten
fiercely strong
the student
became the master
go cower away
sleep fitfully in your lair
knowing you are
accepted but not welcome

I know you want to be friends
I have enough friends
I'm sure you do too
all my friends seem to
know who you are

no longer am I
afraid of you
for I see that
you are in disguise

you are my insecurities
disguised as anxiety
you are my fears
disguised as obsession
I see you
as you are

I accept you
and reject you
all at once
I thank you
and deny you
in one breath

you can hang around
all you want
but I promise you
things will be different

I know your fears
I see your weaknesses
I will make you feel
as unwelcome here
as you tried to make me
I am taking myself back
you can leave.

ELEMENTS

She is the type that
will ask you how you're feeling
when she is at rock bottom
because no matter what
she wants to help

she is the kind that
will ask you what you need
when she has been crying alone
for days wishing secretly
someone would help

she is the one that
will be first on scene
even if they have
never been there
for her

she is the type that
would not be bothered by
us talking about her because
she is too busy worrying what
she thinks about herself
            aren't we all a little like her?

For All/Forever
And so she wept
she wept
and roared and sobbed and heaved
she wept
for all the women who will not weep
for the men who could not cry
she wept
for the mothers who will never be mothers
for the stories that will never be told
she wept
until she trembled
broke apart into stardust
reassembled
into a constellation of grace
she swept herself out of this life
to watch over us forever

ELEMENTS

As I am forced to
look inside
                I am baffled by
the mess I find
I tried so hard to
                keep a neat space
to tidy and clean
not only as needed
                I wanted to resemble
perfection.
                A false belief
                      created by my mind
                        to taunt me
            it haunts me
                    that I was not able to
                    keep my mind stable
            long enough to
                    keep it clean and tidy.

Have I failed
myself or the world
                by not living up to
these impossible visions
my mind creates
                of an ideal life
a mind without strife
can I fail if
                there is no winning?

She is unyieldingly strong
formidable
sturdy as an ice bridge
weathering the fiercest of winter storms
she is shaped by her conditions

she is unwaveringly beautiful
radiant
calm as the rapids
when she looks at you with her crystal clear stare
she is seeing your soul

she is unnecessarily clever
sharp
you will often feel
sword-like words edging into her speech
as she attempts self-defense

beneath the strong
under the beauty
below the clever
lies a world of agony and sorrow
of extraordinary suffering

she created this strength
from within herself with
slow, painful, honest work;
radiant, bone-chilling power
is not purchased from any store

Elements

when you see her
make sure to be gentle
approach
as you would a wild animal
for she is stranded,
balancing between two worlds

be gentle
with this Wild Woman
give her your heart
before revealing your weapon
she might just
love you yet

I try to hide
from myself
it is not that easy
each moment
doing all I can
to forget
my circumstances
each moment
trying to move
further away
from the pain
that plagues me
each moment
trying to remember
that everything is
temporary
this too will end
just as all the
suffering and joy
I have felt in the past
has come to an end
if I can get through
this moment
I can get through anything
   living one moment at a time

ELEMENTS

There were many times
I wanted to give up
I felt hot anger
boiling deep down
in a place I would rather not go

it became a void
too wide to cross
me on one side
my life on the other
neither of us knowing where to go

the sadness I felt
weighed me down like
a pure cast iron fence
that separated me
from my vitality

I still do not know
how to trick these challenges
that life tucks under my feet
for me to trip on
in the deathly black of night
> *but I will never give up completely*

Here we are
For fuck's sake
be proud of yourself
if you are here
reading this

you have made it
through every moment
you thought was
going to be
impossible

you have made it
past every obstacle
someone used to
try to slow
you down

for shit's sake
be happy with yourself
if you are here
breathing
you have done it

everything you thought
you could not do
everything you thought
you would fail at
you did it

celebrate yourself
for being a wicked badass
an unstoppable champion
a fearsome rebel
of your own mind

As the crisp winter air
pressed in around me
with each step further
into the forest
I began to see clearly
for the first time in my life
an unearthly shadow
of myself stretched out
on the midnight snow
in front of me
as behind me shone
my guardian angel
my sister the moon
she whispered
in a language
neither of us knew
guiding me
into a light that
illuminated the truth

Moon Shadow

How Love Feels Today
Have you told yourself
"I love you" today?
Have you given yourself
a hug today?
Go do it
right now
what are you waiting for?
It is the perfect moment
to love yourself
any way
that you can

Softly Falling into Myself

It took many late nights of unproductivity and mental exploration to begin to recognize how much work I had done already. Seeing clearly that I did not love myself was a huge weight off my shoulders; now I had a starting point. As I continued to explore my mind, I tried my best not to be terrified of what I might find. Over many nights, with many tries, I found ways to identify that I had begun to love myself. Once again, it was choice making time. I was faced with a decision of how to treat myself, of whether or not to accept this offer of love being so graciously placed on the table. Deep down I knew my heart was capable of this love, but the question now was if my *mind* was capable of accepting this love. Tearing down this barrier between my mind and heart would open a floodgate which could never be closed. If I agreed to let in this love, there was no turning back. I knew it would be worth it, and fought against the doubt creeping in. I was making the choice between what was easy and what I knew to be right for myself. **I decided I was worthy of all the love in the world, but nobody would believe me unless I showed them how.** I stepped out of my own way and began smashing walls down. Making space inside myself for more love and a new type of light, I swayed under the moonlight of this newfound love. It was painful, letting go of all I had grown so used to. It was challenging, remembering not to let myself fall back into old habits. With steady slowness I flowed down the river of my soul and set up camp in my heart. It will take time but eventually I hope to call it home.

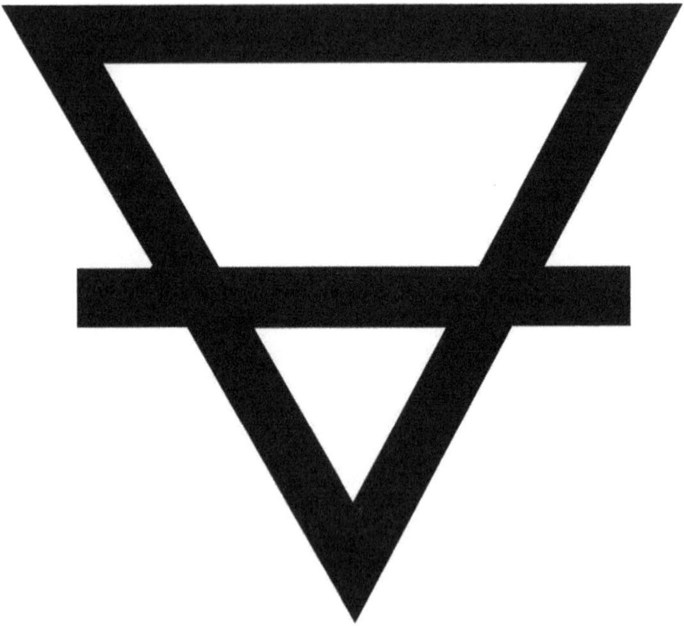

EARTH

Returning

*Once again
in stillness
I feel a pull
rooting deeply
into my being
into my soul
curling up
in a familiar place
connecting to
my past
present
and future self
taking a moment
to speak gratitude
for the journey
the struggle
the hurting
the learning
all of it leading
back to a home
I never knew
I had.*

I Before You
Darling let's get one thing straight
do not think
that I do not love you
just because I love me more

if I did not love me
I could not love you
I'm not being selfish
by prioritizing myself

you are being selfish
by thinking that I
am somehow neglecting you
by taking care of myself

Don't you do the same?
Don't you love you more?
You should
the I always comes before the you

Elements

People may not
remember
the details
of the time
you were there
for them
but they sure as hell
will remember
the time
you were not

I don't want to talk
we can just sit, or walk
and maybe hold hands
or not
I don't have much
to talk about
so I will keep my mouth
shut and take a deep
breath out
I will see how it feels to
enjoy our time just
me and you with
nothing much to do
silent lovers

Lucky Potion
Tell me,
from which cup
did you think
you had to drink
to solve
all your problems at once?

> Did you run into a rabbit
> or a girl named Alice
> perhaps?

Small Town Problems
I can't help but be amused by
the endless whine of passersby
who try to pretend they're not
obsessing over what
he's driving or who
she's talking to

so consumed by
the actions of the neighbours
but we don't know their names, sir
we just want to know
why their fence is so high.

Don't we have better ways
to spend our days than
watching her or him or them?
Keep your eyes on your yard
your weeds are showing

Elements

You can take comfort
in the thought that
everything you have ever
loved
hated
purchased
received
won
lost
cried over
screamed about
will return to the earth
just like you

    stop sweating the little shit

Be wary of those
who are wary of
your heart
your mind
your soul

be wary of those
who are wary of
themselves
their hearts
minds souls

the human mind
is the only creature
with the ability
to reflect upon
its own existence

those who do not
know themselves
are most terrifying
of all creatures
known to mankind

use your mind
to question the minds
of those who find
your courageous heart
weary and dreary

those of soft mind
unaware of their humanness
are the most sinister
of all
humans

Only make room
for the ones who
crave you
love you
make room for you

you will learn
how it feels
when they are
with you for
their own gain

let in those
who put the fools
that do you wrong
right back where
they belong

you will learn
how it feels
to be craved
to be loved
let them in

Elements

You say *people should*
you say *why do people*
you say *can you believe people*
then you do all the things
you say *they should not*
you *do not understand*
you *cannot believe*

Can you believe
people do things
they tell others
they should not?
Because you do.
Believe it.
         I think they call that hypocrisy

Easy Ain't Right
These days it does not seem to matter
the size of your heart
your ability to be honest
your capacity for truth
so long as you have
a teeming bank balance
and a stellar online following
according to someone
you are doing it right
it does not matter
what you are saying
buying or selling
if people are listening
you must be doing
something right

> *What happened to doing*
> *the right thing?*

ELEMENTS

I do not know
what other language
to speak
to get through to you
I pour my heart out to you
break open
shatter apart
your empty response
hangs thickly in the air
I feel more loved by
the static between us
than by your pathetic
attempt at loving me

What else am I supposed to say
when every time I open my mouth
you have already decided
how you feel about
what I am thinking
or feeling
you say I know myself best
and then suggest a half-assed guess
that I would never attempt
you say do what is best for me
and then make me feel guilty
when I take time for me
that's (good) advice
I guess
        I do not know how to love you

Sandra Cooper

Pay yourself
with a moment
of slowing down
in a world where
being too busy
is a status symbol

Yes, you will be fine
without that toxic relationship
without that addiction
if you let go of trauma
if you forgive someone
if you forgive yourself

Yes, you will be great
when you're brave
when you let go
of your attachment to
the version of yourself
that is less than

Girl, you will fucking thrive
after you accept love
after you lay down your shield
once you walk away
from everything holding you back
from loving yourself

Honey, you can do this
if you can love
if you can laugh
after what
you have lived,
you can love *yourself*
> ***of course you can***

Same Human
You are so similar
to them
to her
to him

watch how your hearts beat
hear how your lungs breathe
feel how your hands touch
you are so similar

if it were not for
those seven pesky layers
of skin that we
dress up and paint,

we would never be able
to tell each other apart

With each step
>   I get further from
>   >   the memories and
>   >   >   feelings that haunt me

with each step
>   I get closer to
>   >   a fresh and new
>   >   >   version of me

with each step
>   I get stronger
>   >   and more firmly
>   >   >   rooted in my steps

Hiking into my soul

Silent Mystic
Allow yourself to feel
be open to being you
feel the danger in your wild eyes
taste the fire of your sworded tongue

step into the realm
of endless possibilities
perspective grows in the
shadows of discomfort

pay attention to your patterns
let in the unfamiliar
the ghosts of your past
can define or deny you;
your choice lies ahead
an infinitely tined fork in the road

step step listen
breathe in the air here
taste your wildness
be afraid of your own greatness
and then step into it

be braver than you are
let go of the unknown
open yourself to
your own deep mystery
rooted in the foundation

ELEMENTS

of feeling inadequate
you are too much
let yourself in
feel your limitlessness
greet the silent mystic
waiting patiently in your shadows

Sandra Cooper

Always remember:
what was therapeutic
to read
was therapeutic
to write
express your gratitude

Living Faster than Time
I feel each tick
each tock of the clock
time is playing games
tapping me on
the shoulder

every moment
reminding me she is there
chasing me
standing over me
she steps in my shadow

pulling me back
into her dark past
I do anything I can
to beat the clock
to move faster than time

so I stop feeling it
slowing me down

Pain is not only unpleasant
>*it is also a good teacher*

Fear is not only uncomfortable
>*it is also a great mirror*

Anxiety is not only a monster
>*it is a motivator*

Perception is everything
>*you can transform*

your perspective
>*and start your evolution*

Acknowledge your pain as a teacher

see your fear as a mirror

let your anxiety motivate you

into a new age of

self love

    self acceptance

        glory

            beauty

Let the hard work begin

And then I remembered
forgetting is a natural process
like skin scarring
like bones brittling

forgetting how to love
was just an extension of that
forgetting how to care
was a deepening of the natural process

what once was easy
became a complete mystery
what once took no thought
was now inconceivable

tides turn
earth reshapes itself
moons fade and return
I will come back again

A thick vibrant rainbow
after a miserable storm
that's what you are

Elements

Without stones thrown
at women before me
there would not be
a path for me

were it not for
the breaking of
my ancestor's fragile bones
mine would still be broken

without the oppression of
countless generations before me
I could not claim
to live so freely

      we have come a long way
      but we have a long way to go

You are not failing
you are **trying**

you are not losing
you are **learning**

you are not hopeless
you are **starting fresh**

you are not broken
you are **being rebuilt**

In this moment
I am here
a living, breathing, autonomous being
I am here

I have a story
an age
a family
I came from somewhere
I have been other places

I have feelings, plans, and stories
I have abilities and disabilities
I have possessions and desires
I have fears, doubts, and things to get excited about

I am here
living
breathing
trying my best

I have stories
that will make you believe
in a better life for yourself
that will make you want to
close your eyes forever
that will make your
skin crawl with delight and fear

I'm not afraid
to face my battles head on and fight
to wear my scars, visible and bright
to share my stories and yell them loud

Everything I know
I learned from another
everything I love
I learned from another
everything I fear
I learned from another

Whether you are climbing a mountain or having a meltdown
this is your story
to write
to tell
to share

In this moment
be the person you know best
make yourself proud of all you do
be a friend to yourself first

In this moment
love yourself
despite the weight of the world
trying to make you believe you're unlovable

ELEMENTS

In this moment
breathe
try
do your best (and fuck the rest)

Back to Basics

It took a lot of surrendering. It took a lot of remembering. For months I tried and failed and tried again to be my own best friend, my own ally in the front lines against my mind. I was winning a few battles but certainly losing the war. I processed and reflected after each fight, taking notes, and modifying my strategy. I breathed and raged and stormed and flowed and left remnants of myself every step of the way. Until I no longer existed. Until I stopped breathing and raging and storming and flowing I stopped. Completely. As a phoenix must burn to be reborn, I was experiencing my own waking death. I felt like giving up so many times, and each time the test got harder I got stronger until I stopped thinking about giving up. I had somehow - and it was nothing short of a miracle how I did it - overcome the hardest part and convinced myself that holding on to hope was worth it. That a new birth, a new path, whatever awaited me, would absolutely most certainly be better than what I was living now. I had to let go. I had to let go. I had to let go of everything that anchored me in reality. I had never known my ability to trust until I had to jump, both feet, into an unknown, eyes closed, trusting that I could guide myself back home. I had to unlearn everything that had gotten me into that mess in the first place. I had to unlearn my patterns and processes of believing I was worthless. There was so much letting go I felt myself unraveling into a messy tangle of threads and wires, exposing parts of me that needed to be soldered and remodeled. I felt naked, a type of naked that I was not used to or comfortable with. Piece by piece I had to put myself back together. I had to start with the basics, going back to everything I knew, one by one, and relearning it. No, it was not easy. Yes, I still made mistakes and got hurt. But the beautiful thing about this life is that the more you do not give up on, the more you get to experience. **The more you do not give up the more you grow.** The more you grow the more of life you get to see and then you have more cool stories to tell. But you have to let yourself survive. I had to let myself survive. I went back to basics, rebooted myself, and learned how to find my way back home.

Sandra Cooper

ELEMENTS

Omniverse

*As I observe
my orbit
through this
strange land
I cannot help
but notice
that I seem
to live
in my own
reality.
In that moment
I realize
that everyone
lives in their own
reality and
we are
seeking guidance from
the universe
when really
it is
a multiverse
and it exists
uniquely within
each of us.*

I do not live in your world
the one filled with
new handbags and
matching socks,
manicures and
sculpted eyebrows
just like you do not
live in my world
of making minimum wage and
buying used clothes and
spending more on
prescriptions than I do on
feeding myself so
the next time
you want to comment
on my appearance
maybe consider
that more goes through
my mind in the morning
than how to present myself
to a world full of people
who do not know my story
and are going to judge me anyway
what goes through
my mind in the morning
is how to stay alive
how to avoid the knives
in my eyes
that betray my mind

Elements

and try their hardest
to convince me
that the fight
is too much
maybe consider
before you comment on
how someone looks
that more runs through
their mind in the morning
than how they look
you do not live
in their world
and we should all be
grateful for only having
our own battles to fight
without creating more
for those around us

When I look back
at where I started
and how far I have come
if I had known
how far I would
have to trek

the ghosts I would meet
the demons I would battle
the storms I would weather
the rivers I would cross
the peaks I would reach

I do not know
if I could have
convinced myself
to take the first step
sometimes it is better
not knowing
what lies ahead
otherwise we may
never start the journey
but if I had never

met the ghosts
battled the demons
weathered the storms
crossed the rivers
and *reached* the peaks

ELEMENTS

I would have never
fallen in love with myself

Dissolved
From one day to the next
my reality dissolves
blurring into one stream
of half-faded memories
swirling down the creek
of my past and future at once
I watch as my life
blossoms and unfolds before me
with all the unpredictability
of a bud on a new flower
here I am waiting
for the lesson to come
not realizing
I am living the lesson
each moment

there is nothing
to wait for
the experience
is happening now

Elements

Try not to get upset
when you get
what you asked for
it will always show up
in disguise

I am still learning
how to love myself
when I do not like myself

I am still trying
to appreciate myself
when I do not value myself

I am still practicing
how to be human
one day at a time

forgive my imperfections (*you have them too*)

Elements

Today's To-Do List:
Love yourself

I thought I was done
being taught lessons
how naïve of me
to believe
that after 25 years
I had learned
all I needed to know
to carry me through
the next 50
I was ignorant
in my belief
that the hard part
was behind me
maybe that was why
life reminded me
of my tenuous connection
so I would stop
taking for granted
all I had learned
up until now

the learning is never done

ELEMENTS

I have taken
many trips
around the world

I have seen
many strange
lands and people

nothing taught me
more than
the journey inward

hesitant and afraid
I embarked
into forgotten territory

it was the
hardest
best
most liberating
trip of my life

Begin Within
You do not need
new clothes
fake eyelashes
a diet
to change who you are

you need
to accept yourself
to put down your shield
to find your power
to claim your space

love begins within
polish your heart
until you see
your stunning reflection
sparkling back at you

It is fine
that you got lost
in the hurt
and the pain

it is okay
that you didn't feel
like you were worth
carrying on

it is wonderful
that you learned
how to keep going
despite all that fear

you are never stuck
never lost completely

*your soul always knows
which way to go*

It slapped me like a wall of wind
I love myself
then another
I accept myself

these feelings swirled around me
warming me like a fire
I love myself
I accept myself

raindrops began to fall
I love myself
quenching my eternal thirst
I accept myself

I knelt to the earth
I love myself
scooper her up in my hands
I accept myself
and buried my face in her warmth

I love myself
I accept myself

she whispered these words back to me
and then before I knew it
we were shouting
yelling in pure bliss

Elements

I AM LOVED
I AM MORE THAN ENOUGH
I AM GORGEOUS
I AM WORTHY

together we burned
we rained
we sang our truth
we danced our stories

Mother Earth and me
united again
breathing as one
together into the infinite

I was home
in her arms
her arms which were
really my arms

I love myself
we breathed together
I accept myself
we danced together

into a new dream
together we moved
away from the pain
together we swayed

again I dropped
to my knees and prayed
to the sky above
and the ground below

and all around
which had saved me
I prayed for myself
and my continued healing

my journey is far from over
the earth held me close
my story is far from over
the stars fell gently around me

I danced under the moonlight
alone and worthy
my bare skin glowing
my new life beginning

ELEMENTS

You are fine
he told me
as he rocked me gently
wiping my tears

remember what you are made of
he reminded me
take those deep breaths you know how to
feel that heartbeat you know is so strong

reminders
small moments
breaths
smiles

these got me through
there was never a moment of clarity
nothing ever clicked
I never had a eureka

all I did
was slow down
look for small moments
deep breaths
true smiles

and I hold them close
they are my medicine
they are what heals me

Of course you should keep going
of course it will be worth it
you can't see it now because you're too zoomed in
everything looks terrifying from that close

Zoom out
zoom out until you see beauty
zoom out until you see this great blue rock we are spinning on
zoom out until you see the whole cosmos

The entirety of space
the ether
eternal *space*, empty and endless
feel the vastness
hold on one moment longer

The air begins to form
soft *air* all around, hugging you close
feel the softness
hold on one moment longer

The air moves, becoming fire
transforming *fire*, burning away your past
feel the heat
hold on one moment longer

ELEMENTS

The fire melts into water
flowing *water*, cooling and revitalizing you
feel the calm
hold on one moment longer

The water hardens, becoming earth
grounding *earth*, holding you still
feel the support
you have arrived

Feel these elements lifting you, carrying you,
grounding you
they are always with you
when holding on feels impossible, zoom out
zoom out and find yourself

Find yourself among the elements
reach down deep and feel your heartbeat
it will always remind you, *it's worth it to hold on.*

Taking Life for Granted

It was not until I was alone in those quiet moments that I realized all I had lost. Not in a tragic way but in a liberating way. I had lost my connection to a life I had outgrown. I lost connections to people who had outgrown me. I lost a belief system that made me doubt myself and squashed my potential. There was so much to be grateful for along this journey of loss. I had just been going about it all wrong. Instead of mourning the loss of all I had let go of, I wanted to celebrate all I had learned. It did not take much time at all for me to realize all I had accomplished and regained through this period of suffering. One thing that stood out for me in particular as I reflected was how much I had been taking for granted. Any one of these losses could have been reason enough for me to zip up my miserable suit and surrender to my fate of being a lost cause. And you know what? I would have been. I am where I am because of the choices I made. Once more for the people in the back. *I am where I am because of the choices I made.* There is no fancy spell I've been casting or a magic potion I've been snarfing down backstage. It took a good dose of honest hard work to get my life back on track. It took a lot of stumbling and unsexy, diligent practice building to learn to love myself again. It took courage I did not know I had, and strength I mustered up from generation upon generation of ancestors. With the help of a lot of people around me, the moon, my breath, this notebook, and my inner voice, I persevered. **One fucking brutally slow painful step at a time I walked forward.** I never stopped because I saw what I had given up and I did not want to go back. I would never take myself for granted again. Never again would I be unappreciative of my life. I had learned too much to go back. Me, myself and I had been through too much together. And we were better off for it. Oh, baby were we better off.

Acknowledgments

No matter how much I insist on being independent, I inevitably find myself surrounded by a team of genuine supporters, cheerleaders of sorts, who never let me give up on myself. In addition to those mentioned in the gratitude, the list of people who have influenced and encouraged me could run nearly the length of this book. To everyone who has supported me through this journey, my utmost appreciation goes to you for sticking with me through dark times and giving me reasons to smile so often. For the support, the hugs, the laughs, the dinners, the onesies, the shared tears, the walks, the talks. For everything. This book is as much for you as it is for me....

To the reader

I cannot adequately express my appreciation for your support. This book holds pieces of my soul that I never knew I would be able to share and yet somehow knowing that it could impact your life makes me want to publish a thousand books of poetry. Thank you for agreeing to this journey with me. May these words provide you with some sense of comfort on lonely days, a spark of light on dark nights, or even a tickle of joy when you need it most. I encourage you to hold on, to dig deep, to love yourself as only you know how. These words are for you as much as they are for me.

About the Author

Sandra Cooper is a Canadian artist, yoga instructor and nature enthusiast. The first story Sandra remembers writing was at 7 years old when her cousin was born - it was an 11 page tome describing in detail every aspect of the evening. From that day forth she can only ever remember turning to pen and paper in moments of joy, sadness, to seek comfort, and to sort through confusing emotions.

Throughout her life, Sandra has faced ongoing physical and mental health challenges, and has always found writing to be a useful outlet for the associated frustrations and confusions surrounding chronic illness and pain. Through her social media and blog posts she has been open and honest about her experience with chronic pain, and has always found it therapeutic, both for her and others, to share her journey. She continues to inspire those around her through her powerful poetry.

Ten percent of book sales will be donated to a local women's shelter. Visit domesticpeace.ca to find out more.

Connect with the author:
Facebook: Cooper Poetry
Instagram: cooper.poetry
Website: cooperpoetry.com

Elements

Elements

CPSIA information can be obtained
at www.ICGtesting.com
Printed in the USA
JSHW012101230720
6879JS00001B/1

9 781715 240684